A CLOSER LOOK AT LIVING THINGS

PLANT PARTS

BY STEFFI CAVELL-CLARKE

KidHaven PUBLISHING

Published in 2017 by
KidHaven Publishing, an Imprint of Greenhaven Publishing, LLC
353 3rd Avenue
Suite 255
New York, NY 10010

Designer: Drue Rintoul
Editor: Grace Jones

Cataloging-in-Publication Data

Names: Cavell-Clarke, Steffi.
Title: Plant parts / Steffi Cavell-Clarke.
Description: New York : KidHaven Publishing, 2017. | Series: A closer look at living things | Includes index.
Identifiers: ISBN 9781534520691 (pbk.) | ISBN 9781534520707 (library bound) | ISBN 9781534521124 (6 pack) | ISBN 9781534520714 (ebook)
Subjects: LCSH: Plants–Juvenile literature. | Plant anatomy–Juvenile literature.
Classification: LCC QK641.C38 2017 | DDC 571.3'2–dc23

Printed in the United States of America

CPSIA compliance information: Batch #CW17KL: For further information contact Greenhaven Publishing LLC, New York, New York at 1-844-317-7404.

Please visit our website, www.greenhavenpublishing.com. For a free color catalog of all our high-quality books, call toll free 1-844-317-7404 or fax 1-844-317-7405.

CONTENTS

Words that look like **this** can be found in the glossary on page 24.

WHAT IS A PLANT?

Earth is home to many living things. All living things need water, air, and sunlight to grow and survive. Plants, animals, and humans are all living things.

A DOG IS A LIVING THING.

A SUNFLOWER IS A LIVING THING.

A BOOK IS A NONLIVING THING.

4

Trees, shrubs, herbs, grasses, ferns, and mosses are all different types of plants that can be found on Earth. Some plants have flowering parts, and others do not. Even though plants may look different from one another, many still share the same parts.

PLANT PARTS

Most flowering plants have roots, a stem, leaves, and flowers. Each of these plant parts has a **function** that helps keep the plant alive and healthy.

FLOWER

LEAF

STEM

ROOTS

Leaves make food for the plant.

Roots hold the plant in the ground and **absorb** water and **nutrients** from the soil.

The stem holds the plant up.

Flowers produce **pollen** and seeds.

SEED

New plants grow from seeds. Many seeds
are blown away from plants by the wind and
become buried in the soil. For a seed to grow,
it needs water from the rain and warmth
from the sun. Once it has enough water and
warmth, it will start to **germinate**.

Seeds come in different shapes and sizes. For example, poppy seeds are very small, while the horse chestnut tree produces big seeds that have spiky green shells around them.

HORSE CHESTNUT SEEDS

SUNFLOWER SEEDS

POPPY SEEDS

ROOTS

As the seed splits open, a root begins to grow downward from the seed. The roots have important functions that help the plant grow. One of the functions of the roots is to absorb water and nutrients from the soil.

SOIL

SEED

NUTRIENTS

WATER

ROOT

As the plant grows, extra roots develop to absorb more water and nutrients. Most roots grow underneath the surface of the soil and **anchor** the plant to the ground. This provides a strong base, which helps stop the plant from blowing away in the wind.

SHOOTS

Out of a seed grows a tiny shoot. This is called a seedling, and it sprouts through the soil upward toward the sunlight. The seedling is the first plant part that grows toward the sun. The light from the sun gives the new plant the **energy** it needs to grow.

SUN

SEEDLING

SOIL

ROOTS

12

As the seedling continues to grow, it develops more shoots that begin to produce leaves and flowers.

SHOOT

THE GROWING STAGES OF A SEEDLING

STEM

The seedling develops a stem as it continues to grow above the soil. The stem supports the whole plant and holds the leaves up to the sun so they can absorb as much sunlight as possible.

STEM

The stem connects the roots to the other plant parts. It **transports** water and nutrients from the roots to all the other parts of the plant, such as the leaves. Without the stem, the plant would not be able to survive.

NUTRIENTS

WATER

LEAVES

As the plant grows, it starts to develop leaves. Leaves grow from shoots that branch out from the stem. The function of a leaf is to make food for a plant, which it needs to survive.

The leaf makes food for the plant by absorbing **carbon dioxide** from the air and **energy** from the sunlight. Leaves are often large and thin, which helps them absorb as much sunlight as possible.

SUNLIGHT

CARBON DIOXIDE

17

FLOWER

Many plants grow one or more flowers. A flower starts as a small bud that grows from a shoot and opens up. The flower has many different parts, and some of them produce pollen and seeds.

PETAL

STAMEN

The petals protect the delicate plant parts inside, such as the stamen. The stamen produces pollen for the plant, which is used to make new seeds. The seeds can be blown away from a plant by the wind.

SEEDS

NOT ALL FLOWERS HAVE PETALS.

TREES

BRANCH

LEAF

BARK

TRUNK

A tree is a very large plant. It has a large stem called a trunk, which is covered in a tough layer of bark. The bark helps protect the tree from animals and extreme weather. A tree also has branches, which usually have many leaves on them so they can absorb as much carbon dioxide and sunlight as possible.

Very large trees often have thick roots to anchor the plant upright in the soil. Larger trees need to absorb more water and nutrients than smaller trees.

WATER

NUTRIENTS

LET'S EXPERIMENT!

Do you know what seeds need to grow?
Let's find out!

You will need:

TWO CLEAN, SHALLOW TRAYS

PAPER TOWELS

GARDEN CRESS SEEDS

WATER

TOP TIP
- - - - - - -
ASK AN ADULT TO HELP YOU!

Step 1

Place a thick layer of paper towels in the bottom of each tray. Label the trays A and B. Wet the paper towels in tray A. Cover both trays with the seeds.

Step 2

Put tray A in a warm room next to a window.

Step 3

Place tray B in the refrigerator, so it has no warmth or light.

Step 4

After five days, some seeds will have started to grow. Which tray did the seeds grow in? Can you see how the trays are different?

TOP TIP
- - - - - - - -
MAKE SURE THAT YOU ADD A LITTLE WATER TO TRAY A TO KEEP THE SEEDS MOIST.

Results:

Your experiment will show you that seeds need light, warmth, and water to grow. If they do not have all of these, they will not grow into healthy plants.

23

GLOSSARY

absorb to soak something up

anchor to hold something down

carbon dioxide a colorless gas found in the air

energy the power to work or act

function a specific action

germinate to begin to grow

nutrients substances taken in for growth and health

pollen yellow dust found in flowers

transports moves something from one place to another

INDEX